a cook-book!
Hope it can
help with some
goodies. Love
AL

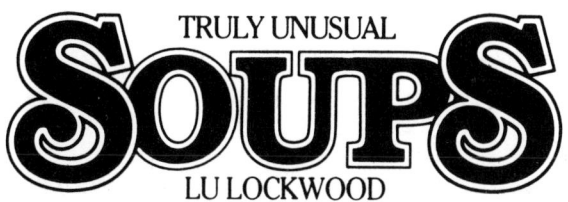

TRULY UNUSUAL SOUPS

LU LOCKWOOD

The Globe Pequot Press

Other books by Lu Lockwood

Cooking with Beer
Cooking with Scotch
Cooking with Game
Her Ladyship's Cook Book
Soups for all Seasons #1
Soups for all Seasons #2

TX
757
.L64

© 1977 Lu Lockwood
All rights reserved
Library of Congress Catalogue Card No. 77-088839
ISBN: 0-87106-091-4
Printed in the United States of America

TEN COMMANDMENTS FOR GREAT SOUPS

1. Read over each recipe carefully, before starting to prepare it. Each recipe will serve four.

2. Assemble all the necessary ingredients before you begin your soup.

3. Always use the best soup broth available. Shop in a quality store, buying only their finest concentrated beef, chicken or vegetable broths. Home-made is best. On following pages you will find four soup broth recipes.

4. The *fresh* version of anything always makes the best of everything.

5. Always have on hand—a 2 quart soup pot or saucepan, a wire whisk, a wooden spoon and an electric blender. If a blender isn't available, a strong strainer will do. In such a case, certain hard foods, such as raw potatoes or carrots, will first have to be chopped very fine and then pushed through the strainer.

6. The soup made a day ahead will surpass one made before you're fed.

7. Pay careful attention to each underlined word in the recipe.

8. The use of the word *slightly* in cooking vegetables means that they should be taken from the heat before they become tender—vegetables continue to cook in hot soup and overcooking means soggy vegetables.

9. Remember—A whole meal can be planned around a hearty soup. Serve with black bread, cheese and wine —then watch how they dine.

10. Don't forget—MEN love soup.

BASIC SOUP BROTHS

Beef Broth

    5 pounds veal and beef bones
    4 pounds shin of beef
    4 quarts of water
    2 onions, quartered
    2 parsley roots, sliced
    3 stalks celery with leaves
    4 sliced carrots
    5 sprigs of parsley
    2 leeks
    2 bay leaves
    ½ teaspoon thyme
    ½ teaspoon dill
    2 tablespoons salt
10 peppercorns

Sear meat in large kettle in a little oil. Quickly brown all over and add the rest of the ingredients. Bring to a boil and cover. Skim occasionally. Simmer 4 to 5 hours. Strain.

    Discard everything. Chill until fat congeals. Remove fat. Keep in glass jug in refrigerator or divide and freeze in containers.

Chicken Broth

    6 pound fowl
    6 quarts cold water
    2 carrots, chopped
    2 onions, chopped
    3 stalks celery and leaves, chopped
    2 parsnips, chopped
    2 leeks
    6 sprigs parsley
    1 tablespoon salt
    1 teaspoon pepper

Put fowl in water and cook 1 hour. Add all remaining ingredients, cover and cook 3 hours. Strain and cool until fat congeals. Do not add chicken meat to broth—freeze meat separately. Discard all vegetables. Skim off fat. Place in glass jug or divide and freeze in containers.

Fish Broth

    2 pounds of fish trimmings; heads, bones, etc.
    ¼ cup parsley, chopped
    ½ cup carrots, chopped
    1 large yellow onion, chopped
    1 potato, peeled and chopped
    1 tablespoon parsley, chopped
    1 bay leaf
    3 stalks of celery, chopped
    4 quarts water

Put all ingredients together in large saucepan. Cover and cook over medium heat for 1½ hours. Strain well. Discard everything. Use as base for fish soups. Place in glass jug or divide and freeze in containers.

Vegetable Broth

    2½ quarts of water
    6 large carrots
    2 small turnips, cut into quarters
    1 large onion, cut into quarters
    2 large leeks
    4 stalks of celery
      trimmings from 2 cauliflowers
    3 tablespoons of butter
    2 tablespoons of oil
    2 tablespoons of dried beans,
      soaked overnight
    1 sprig of thyme
    1 bay leaf
    3 sprigs of parsley
    2 teaspoons of salt
    1 teaspoor of pepper

Wash and pare vegetables. Melt butter and oil in saucepan, add vegetables and simmer, stirring continuously for 15 minutes, until vegetables take on a little color. Add ½ quart of water and cook slowly until all liquid is absorbed. Add beans and remaining water and bring to a boil. Then skim; add the parsley, thyme, bay leaf, and salt and pepper. Simmer two hours. Strain and store in glass jars or divide and freeze in containers.

Celery Velouté

1 bunch celery
1 medium onion, thinly sliced
4 cups chicken broth
4 tablespoons butter
4 tablespoons flour
1 cup heavy cream
½ teaspoon celery salt
½ teaspoon fresh chervil, minced
4 teaspoons sour cream
dash nutmeg
salt and freshly ground black pepper

Cut off the root of the celery, remove the leaves, wash and chop into small pieces. Put in a saucepan with onion and chicken broth. Bring to a boil and simmer gently until the celery is slightly tender. Strain the soup, separating the vegetables from the broth. In the saucepan melt the butter, add the flour and mix well. Slowly pour the broth into the flour paste and cook until smooth and thickening. Return celery and onions to the thickened sauce and then add the celery salt, chervil and nutmeg; season to taste. Heat gently. Garnish with sour cream.

Creme Germiny

1 pound fresh sorrel, finely chopped
3 tablespoons butter
2½ cups chicken broth
4 egg yolks
4 tablespoons heavy cream
1 hard-boiled egg
salt and freshly ground black pepper

Wash, drain and finely shred sorrel. Melt the butter in a saucepan and add sorrel. Simmer gently until slightly tender. Add the chicken broth and bring to a boil. Combine the egg yolks and cream, and then beat until frothy. Pour the egg mixture into the hot broth through a strainer. Season to taste. Simmer gently for 3 minutes. Do not let the soup come to a boil! Garnish with sliced hard-boiled egg.

Madrid Tomato Soup

4 ripe tomatoes, peeled and seeded
1 clove garlic, minced
1 onion, chopped
3 tablespoons olive oil
2 tablespoons vinegar
2 tablespoons parsley
2 cups beef broth
½ cup chopped green pepper
½ cup chopped cucumber
½ cup chopped scallions
½ cup garlic croutons
¼ cup chopped peanuts
   salt, pepper and paprika

Place the first 7 ingredients in a blender, blend well and season to taste. Pour into a bowl and refrigerate until very could. Serve in soup bowls and have the green pepper, cucumbers, croutons, scallions and peanuts in individual bowls on the table to be used as garnish as desired.

Carrot Vichyssoise

3 potatoes, sliced
6 carrots, sliced
2 leeks, sliced
1 ham bone
5 cups chicken broth
1 teaspoon sugar
2 cups cream
½ cup finely cut carrot strips
   salt and finely ground pepper

Cook potatoes, carrots and ham bone in chicken broth until vegetables are tender. Put vegetables and broth in blender, discard bone. Add sugar and cream. Salt and pepper to taste, and chill overnight. Garnish with carrot strips.

Swedish Cherry

2 cans pitted bing cherries
½ cup sugar
6 cloves
6 allspice berries
1 slice lemon
2 pieces cinnamon sticks
1 teaspoon salt
2 tablespoons flour
½ cup heavy cream
½ cup white wine
½ cup sour cream
1 orange, quartered

In a saucepan, drain cans of cherries, setting the cherries aside. To the juice, add sugar, cloves, allspice, lemon, cinnamon sticks and salt. Bring to a boil and remove from the heat. Whisk the flour <u>into</u> the cream and then put the cream <u>into</u> the soup. Add the wine and bring to a boil, stirring constantly. Strain. Chill the clear soup thoroughly. Add sour cream to the cherries and mix gently. Add to the chilled soup. Garnish with orange wedges.

Broccoli Soup

1 package frozen chopped broccoli
2 sprigs fresh parsley
¼ cup minced onion
1 tablespoon butter
½ cup cream
3 cups chicken broth
4 thin lemon slices
pinch of basil

Put all ingredients in sauce pan, but lemon slices. Bring to a boil and simmer 20 minutes. Remove from heat, place in blender and blend 1 minute. Return to saucepan and add one tablespoon butter. Heat and serve with lemon slice.

Swedish Caviar Soup

2 cans frozen cream potato soup
1 cup sour cream
1 cup chicken broth
1 small jar Swedish caviar
1 tablespoon chopped parsley

Thaw the potato soup and put into blender with sour cream, chicken broth and ½ jar of the caviar. Blend for 1 minute. Salt and pepper to taste. Serve hot or cold. Garnish with remaining caviar and top with chopped parsley.

Southern Bisque

1 can cream-style corn
2 cups milk
2 large fresh tomatoes
½ cup cream
2 teaspoons butter
4 sprigs parsley
 salt and pepper

Put first 4 ingredients into a blender and blend for 2 minutes. Pour into a saucepan, add butter, and heat. Season to taste and garnish with parsley.

"No Time" Vegetable Soup

¼ pound bacon
½ cup chopped onions
1 can condensed bean and bacon soup
1 can condensed vegetable soup
1 can condensed cream of mushroom soup
3 cans water
1 cup canned whole kernel corn
1 teaspoon basil
 salt and pepper

Chop the bacon in tiny pieces and saute in saucepan with onions. Add canned soups, corn and water and mix well. Heat slowly, stirring constantly. Salt and pepper to taste. Makes a main meal. Serve with hot corn bread.

Clear Mushroom Soup

1 pound mushrooms, washed and sliced
   (save 8 slices for garnish)
4 cups beef broth
4 teaspoons dry Vermouth
   salt and pepper

Put mushrooms on to cook in beef broth over low heat, and cook ½ hour until very tender. Put into blender and blend 2 minutes. Add Vermouth. Salt and pepper to taste and garnish with slices of raw mushroom.

Greek Lemon Soup

4 cups chicken broth
   juice of 1 medium lemon
2 eggs, well beaten
⅓ cup cooked rice
   salt and pepper

Heat chicken broth to boiling point and add the lemon juice. Important: add 1 cup of chicken broth <u>into</u> the eggs, a little at a time, <u>stirring constantly</u>. Now put the egg mixture <u>into</u> the remaining hot broth. Put the saucepan back on the burner for a few minutes and stir briskly over a low heat to incorporate the egg mixture into the broth. Season with salt and freshly ground black pepper to taste.

Almond Cream Soup

¼ pound butter
1 tablespoon of flour
4 cups chicken consomme
1 cup grated almonds
½ cup heavy cream

Melt the butter in soup pot, add the flour and make a roux, slowly add chicken consomme and now grated almonds. Lower heat and simmer 15 minutes. Gradually add the cream stirring constantly. Place soup in the blender and blend one minute.

   Serve hot or cold.

Caldo Gallego

- 1/8 pound dried chick peas
- 1/8 pound sliced spanish sausage (chorizo)
- 1/8 pound sliced salt pork
- 2 tomatoes, peeled and chopped
- 2 cloves garlic
- 1 quart chicken broth
- 1 teaspoon cuminseeds, crushed
- 1/2 pound greens (dandelion is best)
- 1 ham bone
- salt and pepper

Cover the chick peas with water and bring to a boil. Drain and discard the water. Saute the salt pork until lightly brown. Add the sausage and cook until lightly brown. Add chick peas, tomatoes, garlic, ham bone, broth, cuminseeds and browned sausage. Cover, bring to a boil and simmer 2 hours. Add greens and cook five minutes more. Remove the bone. Salt and pepper to taste.

Cape Cod Clam Chowder

- 1/4 pound salt pork, cut into tiny pieces
- 1 cup finely chopped onion
- 3 cups cold water
- 4 cups potatoes, cut into 1/4 inch pieces
- 3 dozen shucked hard shelled clams with their juice, coarsely chopped, or 3/8 ounce cans of chopped clams
- 2 cups light cream
- 1/8 teaspoon thyme
- salt and freshly ground pepper
- 3 tablespoons of butter

Fry the diced pork in heavy 3 quart kettle, stirring constantly for about 3 minutes. Lower heat and stir in onions and cook together for 8 minutes. Add 3 cups water and potatoes. Bring to a boil and then lower heat and simmer until potatoes tender. Add clams, juice, cream and thyme. Heat to almost boiling point. Stir in butter and salt and pepper to taste.

Haddock Chowder

2 lbs. of haddock cut up in small pieces
2 cups of water
4 ounces diced salt pork
2 sliced thin medium size onions
4 sliced thin medium size cooked potatoes
1 Teaspoon salt
1 quart milk
3 tablespoons of butter
2 tablespoons of flour

Simmer the haddock in the water for ten minutes. Drain and reserve the broth. Saute the pork, saute the onion in pork fat, add the flour and mix well until all flour disappear. Slowly add fish broth and milk, cook slowly. Add fish, seasoning and butter.

Sherry Soup

1½ lb. beef cut into small pieces
1 veal knuckle
2 medium size, sliced thin carrot slices
1 medium size, sliced thin white turnip
2 medium size, sliced thin onions
2 quarts of water
¼ teaspoon minced red pepper
salt and pepper
2 cups sherry

Combine all ingredients but the sherry. Place in large kettle, cover, cook slowly for five hours. Cool and refrigerate over night. Next day, skim, remove knuckle. Heat the soup, add the sherry, beat one minute and serve over slices of toasted rye bread with caraway seeds.

The Crab Soup

Remove meat from 12 steamed blue crabs, reserving the roe. In a sauce pan melt 1 tablespoon butter, add 1 tablespoon flour and cook over low heat, remove from heat and add 4 cups scalded milk stirring carefully. Return to heat and stir until smooth, add crabmeat, 1 teaspoon onion juice, ½ teaspoon worcestershire sauce, ¼ teaspoon mace, salt and pepper to taste. Cook slowly 20 minutes.

Divide roe into 6 bowls—add 1 tablespoon sherry to each bowl and scoop hot soup into bowls. Garnish with fresh chopped parsley.

Spinach Consomme

1 pound fresh spinach washed and stems removed and chopped fine
2 cans chicken consomme
6 teaspoons sour cream
salt and pepper

Cook the spinach in the chicken consomme for ten minutes. Cool, blend, season and serve hot with one teaspoon of sour cream per dish.

Easy Avacado Soup

2 cans of condensed potato soup
3 tablespoons of dry sherry
2 ripe peeled avacadoes
2 tablespoons of lemon juice
1 cup of milk
1 cup of cream

Slice 6 pieces of avocado for soup bowls. Set aside.

Place all ingredients in blender, blend well, pour over avacado slices in individual bowls. Refrigerate until very cold.

Easy Clam Soup

1 can of cream of celery soup
1 can of chicken consomme
1 quart clam juice
  chopped chives

Place cream of celery in kettle, dilute slowly, stirring constantly, with the chicken consomme, add the clam juice and the chives. Serve very hot.

Fresh Mushroom Creme

8 tablespoons butter
½ pound fresh mushrooms, peel the caps, wash and slice lengthwise
3 tablespoons flour
2½ cups chicken broth
1 cup milk
  juice of medium lemon
½ cup heavy cream
3 tablespoons fresh parsley sprigs
  salt and freshly ground pepper

Melt 2 tablespoons of butter and saute mushrooms for about 5 minutes over a medium heat. Set aside. In a saucepan slowly melt 6 tablespoons of butter, and then add 3 tablespoons of sifted flour. Mix well. Gradually add chicken broth, milk, lemon, and heavy cream. Add mushrooms and parsley; salt and pepper to taste.

Soup a la Napolean

Saute 2 pounds of sliced thin onions in ½ cup butter, when cooled whirl in a blender. Pour into a sauce pan, add 2 cups of Pouilly Fuisse, 2 cups of chicken broth, heat, do not boil. Over low heat add 1 cup grated swiss cheese, stirring until blended.

    Sprinkle with chopped parsley, serve with croutons.

Clam Stew

2 slices of bacon, cut into small pieces
1 large onion, minced
1 clove of garlic, minced
1 small green pepper, minced
4 stalks of celery, chopped fine
1 carrot, chopped fine

In soup kettle saute bacon for a few minutes add all vegetables and cook until tender.

Meanwhile:

1 quart of shucked chopped clams and liquid
3 tablespoons of butter
1 tablespoon of flour
3 large diced potatoes
½ teaspoon oregano
2 teaspoons of salt
¼ teaspoon of pepper
dash cayenne
½ cup chopped parsley
1 can peeled tomatoes (1 lb. 12 ounces)

Add butter to cooked vegetables then smooth flour into mixture then all remaining ingredients, cover, turn heat low and simmer until potatoes tender.

Molly's Left Over Salad Soup

If you have 2 cups of leftover green salad and an adventurous but sometimes parsimonious spirit, saute a sliced peeled potato in 3 tablespoons of butter. When the potatoes are golden, add 2 cans of chicken broth and cook 15 minutes. Add the salad remains (don't drain the dressing) and your favorite herb (dill, basil, oregano, rosemary) and simmer for another 10 minutes or until the potatoes are tender. Pour the whole thing into your blender and whirl for a couple of minutes. Like nothing else you've ever tasted!

Chicken Almond Soup

2 cans cream of chicken soup
1 cup light cream
1 cup milk
¼ teaspoon almond extract
¼ cup almond slivers
   salt and pepper

Place first 4 ingredients in blender, blend for ½ minute. Place in saucepan, heat gently, and salt and pepper to taste. Garnish with almond slivers.

Quick Super Soup

4 cups beef broth
½ pound sauerkraut
½ pound smoked German sausage

Put sauerkraut and broth on to boil over <u>low flame</u> and simmer ½ hour. Garnish with slices of German sausage.

Early Spring Soup

2 pounds fresh spinach
6 tablespoons butter
1¼ cups cream
2½ cups chicken broth
4 dashes nutmeg
   salt and freshly ground black pepper

Wash the spinach leaves and remove stem and backbone. Make sure they are very clean. Put the butter in a saucepan and melt. Add spinach and simmer gently until tender. Remove from the saucepan and cool. Place in a blender and add the cream and chicken broth, blend well. Return to the saucepan and heat <u>gently</u>. Salt and pepper to taste. Garnish with a dash of nutmeg. Also delicious served cold.

Petite Marmite

- ½ pound corned beef
- 1 oxtail
- 4 chicken wings
- 2 quarts beef broth
- 2 carrots, scraped and cut into sticks
- 2 leeks, cut into slices
- 1 small white turnip, peeled and diced
- 1 onion, sliced
- ¼ cup grated Gruyère cheese
- 2 crusty rolls
- salt and freshly ground black pepper

Place the beef, oxtail and chicken into a saucepan and cover with beef broth. Add 2 teaspoons of salt and cook for 1 hour. Then add all the vegetables and cook for 20 minutes more. Skim the top of the soup. Remove the beef and oxtail, cut them into bite-size pieces and return them to the soup. Season to taste. Serve hot, garnished with Gruyère and thin slices of crusty rolls. This makes a main meal.

Leafy Green Soup

- 3 heads of Boston lettuce
- 6 scallions
- 3 tablespoons butter
- 5 cups chicken broth
- 1 egg yolk
- 4 tablespoons heavy cream
- fried croutons of bread
- salt and fresh ground pepper

Wash lettuce, remove outer leaves and hard core. Wash scallions. Slice both vegetables thinly and sauté them in 3 tablespoons of melted butter. Simmer gently for 10 minutes. Add chicken broth, bring to a boil, reduce heat and cover. Simmer gently for 10 more minutes. Beat the egg yolk and add the cream. Pour hot soup into egg mixture, stirring all the time. Salt and pepper to taste. Serve hot with croutons.

Spring Asparagus Soup

½ pound fresh asparagus
¼ cup onion
5 tablespoons butter
2½ cups chicken broth
3 tablespoons flour
1 cup whipped heavy cream
grated ½ lemon rind
1 tablespoon finely chopped fresh parsley
salt and fresh ground pepper

Peel asparagus with vegetable peeler, removing all stringy outer parts. Cut off tough ends, if necessary. Cut into 1 inch pieces. Combine asparagus with finely chopped onion and add to the chicken broth. Simmer until slightly tender. Put the butter into the saucepan and when it melts add the flour. Remove the asparagus from the broth and add the broth to butter and flour mixture until it thickens slightly. <u>Fold</u> in the whipped cream and lemon rind. Very carefully put the asparagus back into the soup. Salt and pepper to taste. Garnish with parsley.

Green Mountain Chicken

¼ cup chopped onion
¼ cup chopped celery
¼ cup butter
¼ cup flour
3 cups chicken broth
1 cup light cream
1 cup cooked chicken, cubed
½ cup cooked rice
4 sliced green olives
4 sliced pitted black olives
salt and pepper

Brown onions and celery in the butter; add flour and blend well. Add broth slowly, <u>stirring constantly,</u> then add cream, chicken, rice and olives. Simmer 10 minutes. Season to taste. Makes a main meal. Serve with hot old fashion baking powder biscuits.

Pea Soup Diable

2 medium-size cans frozen pea soup, thawed
2 cups rich milk
1 large can devilled ham
1/8 teaspoon hot pepper sauce
1 teaspoon fresh dill
2 tablespoons grated lemon rind
4 teaspoons sour cream
   salt and pepper

Place first 5 ingredients in a blender for 1 minute. Add 1 tablespoon lemon rind, blend 5 seconds. Salt and pepper to taste. Serve hot or cold. Garnish with a teaspoon of sour cream and sprinkle with lemon rind.

Cold Cucumber Soup With Mint

2 large cucumbers
4 scallions
1 tablespoon chopped mint
1 cup chicken broth
1/2 pint sour cream
   salt and freshly ground black pepper

Peel and seed the cucumber. Puree in an electric blender. Then add scallions and 1/2 teaspoon of mint to blender and blend for 2 minutes. Add sour cream, chicken broth, and blend for 1 minute at low speed. Pour into a bowl and season with salt and pepper to taste. Garnish with remaining mint.

Champagne and Crab Soup

1 quart chicken broth
2 teaspoons lemon juice
1 pound flaked fresh crabmeat
1/2 cup heavy cream
1 tablespoon chopped chives
1/2 bottle champagne

Bring the chicken broth to boil and add the lemon juice. Add the crabmeat and boil 10 minutes. Remove from heat and add the cream and chives. Put the saucepan back to simmer for 5 more minutes. Bring the champagne to a boil and add to the soup. Serve at once.

New York Gazpacho Soup

2 cans consomme
3 tomatoes
½ cucumber
2 tablespoons chopped green pepper
1 tablespoon chopped pimento
1 minced garlic clove
1 tablespoon sherry
  salt and freshly ground black pepper

Pour the consomme into a large bowl. Peel the tomatoes and chop into small pieces. Peel, remove seeds and chop the cucumber. Combine all ingredients into the consomme and chill overnight or at least six hours.

Farmhouse Vegetable Soup

½ cup onions, diced
½ cup green beans, cut into small pieces
½ cup potatoes, peeled and diced
1 cup stewed tomatoes
3 cups vegetable broth
¼ cup vermicelli, broken
1 garlic clove
1 teaspoon fresh basil
1 teaspoon fresh thyme
1 teaspoon fresh sage
1 egg yolk
⅛ cup oil
½ cup grated Cheddar cheese
  salt and freshly ground black pepper

Put oil in a saucepan; add garlic, onions, green beans and potatoes. Sauté for 2 minutes. Add tomatoes, broth, basil, thyme, sage, and vermicelli. Bring to a boil and simmer for 20 minutes. Beat the egg yolk and add 1 cup hot soup <u>into</u> the egg mixture and blend well, but very gently. Return the soup and egg mixture to the saucepan, season to taste and garnish with cheese.

Watercress Corn Soup

1 garlic clove, minced
⅓ cup tiny onion rings
¼ cup butter
1½ cups fresh corn, cut off the ears
1 teaspoon salt
½ teaspoon sugar
1 cup water
1½ cups milk
1 cup chopped watercress
2 egg yolks, beaten
½ cup heavy cream
salt and pepper

Sauté the garlic and onion rings in the butter in a saucepan for 3 minutes. Add the corn, sugar and water. Bring to boil and simmer for 15 minutes. Add milk and chopped watercress. Cover and cook for 5 minutes more. Remove from heat and cool. Put into the blender for 1 minute. Return to the saucepan and add the egg yolks, <u>one at a time</u>. Then add the cream and seasonings. Heat and garnish with sprigs of watercress.

Mama's Fruit Soup

3 cups assorted fruits (peaches, plums, apricots, berries, pears and cherries)
4 cups water
2 teaspoons lemon juice
4 tablespoons sugar
2 tablespoons cornstarch
½ cup sour cream
1 tablespoon Kirsch

Wash and cut up fruit, peeling, removing cores and seeds. Place in saucepan and add water, sugar and lemon juice. Cook over low heat for 20 minutes. Mix cornstarch with 2 tablespoons of water and add to fruit, stirring constantly. Cool and refrigerate. Add 1 tablespoon Kirsch and a little more sugar if desired. Garnish with sour cream.

Lobster Stew

¼ cup butter
2 cups lobster meat (1 pound)
½ teaspoon salt
¼ teaspoon paprika
3 cups milk
1 cup heavy cream
1 tablespoon chopped parsley
salt and pepper

Put butter in saucepan, melt, and add 1½ cups lobster meat cut into bite-size pieces. Saute 2 minutes, add milk, then simmer gently 10 minutes. Put cream and the other ½ cup lobster meat in a blender and blend for 1 minute. Pour into saucepan and simmer 5 minutes. Season to taste. Garnish with chopped parsley.

Crab Soup Survey

1 pound crabmeat
1½ cups milk
3 tablespoons butter
2 tablespoons flour
1½ cups heavy cream
⅓ cup Scotch whisky
¼ cup chopped parsley
salt and freshly ground black pepper

Melt the butter gently in saucepan, add crabmeat and sauté carefully for a few minutes. Add 2 tablespoons of flour and mix well. Slowly add the milk and whisky. Simmer for 10 minutes. Whip the cream and fold into the soup. Salt and pepper to taste. Garnish with chopped parsley.

Quick Indian Chicken Soup

2 cans cream chicken soup
1 can milk
2 apples, peeled and cored
½ cup sour cream
⅛ teaspoon marjoram
½ teaspoon thyme
1 teaspoon curry powder
2 teaspoons lemon juice
salt and pepper
4 sprigs watercress

Put all the ingredients but watercress in a blender for 2 minutes. Salt and pepper to taste. Serve hot or cold. Garnish with sprigs of watercress.

Watercress Soup

1 bunch watercress
2 tablespoons butter
1 small onion, sliced
1 large potato, peeled and sliced
2 leeks
1 cup cream
2 cups chicken broth
1 cup milk
  salt and pepper

Chop stems off the watercress and throw away. Chop leaves and set ½ cup aside for garnish. Saute leeks, onion and potato in butter for a few minutes. Add chicken broth and watercress and cook until vegetables are tender. Put everything in the blender and blend 3 minutes. Put soup in a saucepan and add milk, cream and season to taste. Serve hot or very cold. Garnish with remaining watercress.

Iced Carrot Soup

8 carrots, scraped and sliced
2 stalks celery, sliced
1 small onion, sliced
1 small bay leaf
2 cloves
3 cups chicken broth
2 tablespoons chopped parsley
  a few drops of tabasco
½ cup heavy cream
  salt and freshly ground black pepper

Add the first 5 ingredients to the chicken broth and put in a saucepan. Cook over a moderate heat until the vegetables are tender. Remove bay leaf and cloves and put into a blender for 1 minute. Add 2 tablespoons of finely chopped parsley, a few drops of tabasco; salt and pepper to taste. Chill overnight and add ½ cup heavy cream. Garnish with tiny croutons.

Frosted Consomme

2 cans consomme, set in refrigerator until jelly
½ cup sour cream
1 teaspoon anchovy paste
1 teaspoon chopped onion
¼ teaspoon chopped chives

Mix sour cream, paste and onion. Put jelly into 4 champagne glasses. Frost with cream mixture and sprinkle with chopped chives.

Yoghurt Soup

½ cup raisins
3 cups plain yoghurt
½ cup light cream
1 hard boiled egg, chopped
1 small cucumber, peeled, seeded and cubed
¼ cup green onions, chopped finely
1 tablespoon parsley, chopped
1 teaspoon fresh dill, chopped finely
salt and pepper

Soak raisins in cold water for 5 minutes. Place yoghurt in a bowl, add egg, cream, cucumber, onion, parsley and dill. Add raisins and mix carefully. Salt and pepper to taste. Chill in refrigerator for two or three hours.

Salmon Bisque

¼ cup butter
⅓ cup onion, finely chopped
⅓ cup green pepper, finely chopped
⅓ cup celery, finely chopped
3 tablespoons flour
4 cups milk
1 can salmon, drained, deboned and skinned
2 tablespoons chopped pimento
salt and pepper

Melt the butter in a saucepan; add onion, green pepper and celery. Cook until lightly brown. Add the flour; stir into a paste. Remove from the heat; add the salmon, milk and pimento stirring all the time until slightly thick. Salt and pepper to taste. Return to heat and simmer ten minutes.

Callaloo Soup

If you can't find callaloo greens use Swiss Chard.

In a kettle combine 2 lbs. callaloo or chard leaves with 4 cups water, ½ pound of sliced okra, a ham bone with ham on it, 4 scallions everybit, chopped, 1 garlic clove, minced. 1 tablespoon chopped parsley, ½ teaspoon thyme, 1 teaspoon salt and ½ teaspoon pepper. Bring to a boil, cover and simmer 1 hour.

Remove ham bone and cut up all meat and return to soup. Transfer soup, so much at a time to a blender and puree. If the soup is too thick, thin it out with chicken broth. Serve with thick slices of buttered blackbread.

Summer Watercress Soup

- 2 cans of condensed celery soup
- 1 bunch of watercress, washed well and stems removed
- 1 cup milk
- 1 cup cream
- ¼ sliced onion
- ½ teaspoon of salt

Place all ingredients in blender, blend one minute, serve cold with dash of ground cloves.

Chilled Cream Vichyssoise

- 4 leeks, finely sliced
- ¼ cup finely chopped onion
- ¼ cup butter
- 5 medium potatoes, cut up into small pieces
- 1 quart chicken stock
- 1 teaspoon salt
- 2 cups milk
- 3 cups cream

Saute leeks and onion in butter until yellow. Add potatoes, chicken stock and salt. Bring to a boil, cover, reduce heat and simmer until potatoes are soft. Put into blender for one minute, return to heat and add milk. Season to taste. Cool. Add cream and chill thoroughly.

Smoked Turkey Soup

Bones and left over smoked Turkey meat (neck meat, wing meat etc.)
3 chopped fine onions
4 chopped fine celery stalks
1 chopped fine garlic bud
3 chopped fine carrots
2 quarts of water
1 tablespoon farina
1 egg beaten
chopped parsley

Place bones, meat, vegetables and garlic in water. Cover and cook until vegetables are tender. Strain the broth through a double cheese cloth. Discard all vegetables, bones and meat. Add farina and beaten egg and whip until creamy, add parsley.

Summer Salmon Mousse Soup

½ garlic clove, minced
1 small onion, sliced thin
½ green pepper, sliced thin
1 tablespoon butter
1 medium can salmon, skinned and boned
1½ cup milk
¼ teaspoon tabasco
½ cup heavy cream
2 tablespoons sherry
4 slices lemon
salt and pepper to taste

Saute garlic, onions and green pepper in the butter. Add salmon, milk and tabasco, simmer for 15 minutes. Remove from the heat, cool and put in a blender for 1 minute. Mix cream and sherry, and add to the soup. Blend ½ minute more. Salt and pepper to taste. Chill in refrigerator for 2 or 3 hours. Garnish with lemon slices.

Cold Curried Chicken & Pea

1 package frozen peas
1 can milk
1 can of cream of chicken soup
1 teaspoon curry
½ cup heavy cream
   salt and pepper

Heat cream of chicken soup diluted with 1 can of milk. Add frozen peas and cook slowly for twenty minutes. Add cream and seasoning. Place in blender and blend one minute.

   Serve cold.

Hasty Cucumber Soup

1 can of cream of potato soup
1 can of cream of chicken soup
2 peeled and seeded cucumbers
½ cup heavy cream

Put all ingredients into blender—blend well. Add salt and pepper to taste and chill over night. Serve with bowl of sour cream and chopped chives.

Apple and Banana Soup

Bring to a boil 2 cups chicken stock. Add 1 finely chopped apple, 1 banana peeled, 1 peeled and diced potato, 1 chopped onion. Cook covered till ingredients are soft. Strain or put through the blender. Add 2 cups light cream, ½ teaspoon salt, and ½ teaspoon freshly cracked white pepper. Serve hot or cold garnished with 1 teaspoon chopped chives on each serving. Serves 6.

   Note: May add 1 teaspoon curry powder to soup while cooking.

Jellied Clam Broth

3 tablespoons gelatin
¼ cup cold water
4 cups hot Clamato juice
4 lime slices
4 teaspoons sour cream

Mix gelatin with cold water and add hot Clamato. Pour into rimmed cookie sheet and chill until well set. Cut into cubes and pile in wine goblets. Garnish with sour cream and slice of lime.

Quickie Cold Borsch

1 quart prepared borsch
1 can (1 lb.) sliced beets, drained
½ cup sliced thin onions
2 cups sour cream
2 tablespoons of fresh dill
   or 1 teaspoon dried dill

In a blender add borsch, beets, onions, 1 cup sour cream, and half the amount of dill. Blend well, pour into bowl, refrigerate overnight.

Mix 1 cup sour cream with remaining dill, refrigerate overnight.

Serve borsch in stem glasses with sour cream on top.

Carrot and Leek Soup

5 carrots, scraped, washed and sliced
4 leeks, trimmed and sliced
4 cups chicken broth
5 sprigs parsley
½ cup cream
   salt and freshly ground black pepper
4 thin carrot slices

In a saucepan combine carrots, leeks and chicken broth. Cook for 25 minutes. Place soup in a blender and beat until purée. Add the sprigs of parsley and beat for 1 more minute. Chill. Add the cream and seasonings. Garnish with carrot slice.

Creamy Cold Tomato

1 finely chopped onion
6 coarsely chopped tomatoes
½ teaspoon salt
¼ cup water
2 cups bouillon
1 cup heavy cream
2 tablespoons tomato paste mixed well with
   2 tablespoons of flour.

Place first five ingredients in kettle and cook for 15 minutes. Add tomato paste with flour and stir in well, cook 10 more minutes. Place in blender add ½ cup heavy cream and blend well. Chill over night. Beat remaining heavy cream and drop by teaspoon into soup.

Hollandaise Soup

½ small fresh yellow turnip
2 fresh carrots
½ pound fresh peas
½ medium cucumber
2 tablespoons butter
2 tablespoons flour
4 cups chicken broth
2 egg yolks
¾ cup light cream
1 teaspoon sugar
1 teaspoon fresh chopped tarragon
  salt and fresh ground pepper

Peel the skin of the turnip down 1 half-inch deep to remove all bitterness, and cut into tiny cubes. Put the turnip in a saucepan, cover with water and cook for 10 minutes. Scrape and cut the carrots into thin sticks 2 inches long, and add them to the turnip together with enough water to cover carrots. Cook 10 minutes. Add the peas and cucumber and cook 5 minutes more. Then remove from heat, drain and set aside. Place 2 tablespoons of butter in a saucepan, melt and add the flour, mixing well. Then slowly add the chicken broth. Simmer, stirring constantly until it thickens. Turn off heat. Blend the cream in with the beaten egg yolks and strain into the hot sauce. Mix well. Add cooked vegetables, sugar and tarragon; salt and pepper to taste. Serve very hot, but do not reach boiling point.

New York Clam Consomme

2 cups chicken broth
1 cup tomato juice
1 cup canned clam broth
1 large sprig parsley
1 slice onion
½ cup celery tops
4 thin lemon slices
  salt and pepper

Put all ingredients into a saucepan and simmer for 30 minutes. Strain and season with salt and pepper. Serve with lemon slice.

Chilled Garden Tomato Soup

2 pounds ripe tomatoes
1 tablespoon sugar
2 teaspoons salt
½ teaspoon onion juice
½ teaspoon ground cloves
  juice and rind of ½ lemon
½ cup heavy cream
¾ cup boiled or baked ham, shredded
½ cucumber, peeled, seeded and diced
1 tablespoon fresh parsley sprigs
  salt and pepper

Puree the tomatoes in an electric blender. Pass through a strainer. Place in a bowl and add sugar, salt, onion juice, cloves, lemon, ham and cream; salt and pepper to taste. Chill several hours. Garnish with the parsley sprigs.

Consomme Aurora

1½ tablespoons quick-cook tapioca
¼ cup tomato sauce
3 cups chicken broth
½ cup Julienne strips of cooked chicken
  salt and fresh-ground pepper

Combine first 3 ingredients in a saucepan. Cover and cook on medium heat until tapioca is transparent. Salt and pepper to taste. Put strips of chicken into each soup bowl followed by the hot consomme.

Old Fashion Swiss Cheese Soup

4 slices stale bread, crumbled into pieces
1 cup grated Gruyere cheese
2½ cups hot beef broth
⅓ cup white wine
2 tablespoons butter

Using some of the butter, butter a casserole dish, best to use individual casseroles, and make layers of cheese and bread. Pour hot broth and wine over the bread and cheese. Dot with balance of butter and bake in 350 degree oven for 25 minutes.

Potage Chantilly

1 cup cooked green peas
2 tablespoons flour
2½ cups chicken broth
1½ cups milk
2 tablespoons butter
½ cup heavy cream
2 strips bacon, crumbled
salt and pepper

Set aside ⅓ cup of peas and put remaining peas in a blender. Add cream, blend 1 minute. Melt butter in saucepan, add flour and mix well. Slowly add milk, then broth. Stir in puree from blender. Add balance of peas. Salt and pepper to taste. Garnish with crumbled bacon.

Summer Pea Soup

¾ pound shelled peas
1 medium potato
1 medium onion
1 head of lettuce, cut up
2½ cups chicken broth
1 cup heavy cream
juice of ½ lemon
salt and fresh-ground black pepper

Place peas, onion, lettuce and half the chicken broth in a saucepan and bring to a boil. Cover and simmer 15 minutes. Transfer to an electric blender and blend until vegetables are puréed. Return to saucepan; add balance of chicken broth, cream and lemon; then salt and pepper to taste. Serve well chilled.

Cape Scallop Soup

    2 slices lean bacon in tiny pieces
    1 cup thinly sliced potatoes
    2 tablespoons butter
  20 cape or bay scallops
  2½ cups water
    1 tablespoon chopped parsley
    ½ teaspoon thyme
    1 cup fresh sliced tomatoes
    ½ cup cream
    2 tablespoons seasoned breadcrumbs
       dash of ground mace

Cook bacon for 2 minutes, remove and set aside. Add butter, scallops, potatoes, parsley and thyme. Sauté 2 minutes. Add water and cover. Cook very slowly for 20 minutes. <u>Do not boil.</u> Add tomatoes, cook 5 more minutes. Stir in cream, bacon and crumbs; salt and pepper to taste. Sprinkle with mace.

Won Ton Soup

    ½ pound noodle dough
       (purchased or make your own)
    ½ pound ground pork
    1 tablespoon dry sherry
    2 tablespoons soy sauce
 1½ teaspoons salt
    ½ teaspoon sugar
    ¼ teaspoon monosodium glutamate
    3 quarts boiling water
    ½ cup cold water
    3 cups chicken broth
    1 scallion, chopped

Roll out the dough until it is paper thin. Cut into four-inch squares. Mix together the pork, sherry, 1 tablespoon of the soy sauce, one half-teaspoon of the salt, the sugar and the monosodium glutamate. Place 1 teaspoon of the mixture in the middle of each square. Fold over at the center, pressing the edges together. Fold lengthwise again. Pull the corners one over the other and press them together with a little water. When properly folded, the won ton resembles a nurse's cap. Add the wrapped won tons to the boiling water and bring to a boil again to make sure the filling is cooked. Drain and reserve. Heat the chicken broth. Add the remaining soy sauce and salt. Drop the reserved won tons and scallion into the broth and cook 20 minutes. Yield: 16 won tons (4 servings).

Quick Chesapeake Oyster and Chicken

2 cans cream of chicken soup
1 can frozen oyster stew
1 tablespoon butter
1 cup milk
1 cup light cream
  chopped chives
  salt and pepper

Thaw oyster stew and strain. Set the oysters aside. Blend the oyster stew, cream of chicken soup, milk and cream in a blender for 1 minute. Place in a saucepan; add oysters, butter, salt and pepper. Simmer for 10 minutes. Garnish with chopped chives.

Kaassoep

2 cups grated Gouda
¼ cup flour
½ cup butter
3 cups half-and-half milk and cream
½ teaspoon Worcestershire sauce
2 drops Tabasco
1 strip cooked bacon, crumbled
  salt and pepper

Put butter into saucepan over low heat. When melted, add flour and blend well but do not brown. Slowly add cream and milk, stirring constantly until it becomes a smooth creamy mixture. Add the rest of the ingredients and cook over a low heat until it is a creamy, smooth soup. Garnish with crumbled bacon.

White Bean Soup

2 quarts chicken stock
2 cups dry white beans (great Northern)

Bring to a boil, remove from heat and soak 1 hour.

Melt 1 tablespoon of butter. Stir in 1 cup finely chopped onions, 2 leeks cut in pieces. Cut ¼ lb. salt pork cut into tiny pieces add to onions and leeks.

Add the vegetables to beans, mix well, ½ cup white wine, 1 bouquet garni, 1 teaspoon salt, 2 tablespoons chopped parsley. Uncovered and simmer for 2 hours. Discard Garni, check seasoning to taste.

Serendipity

8 tomatoes
1 cucumber, peeled
1 onion, cut up in pieces
⅛ cup lemon juice
salt, pepper, dash of cayenne pepper

Place all in blender and blend 2 minutes. Chill thoroughly. Serve in chilled mugs.

Corn Chowder With A Twist

¼ pound salt pork, cut into tiny pieces
2 tablespoons flour
1 can cream style corn
1 onion, chopped fine
1 whole carrot, sliced thin
1 green pepper, cut into thin strips 1" long
1 teaspoon lemon juice
4 cups milk
4 twists lemon peel
salt and pepper to taste

Place salt pork into a saucepan and simmer slowly for 10 minutes. Add onions, peppers and carrots. Saute until slightly tender. Add flour and mix well. Add lemon juice, milk and corn. Cook for 10 minutes more. Season to taste. Garnish with a twist of lemon.

Laurent Soup

1 garlic clove
1 medium size onion (chopped)
6 peeled ripe medium tomatoes
1 cup beef consomme
2 tablespoons of tarragon vinegar
2 tablespoons of chopped parsley
¼ teaspoon of paprika
¼ teaspoon of salt

Place all ingredients in a blender and blend until smooth. Chill overnight.

Chop 1 small green pepper into small cubes. Mix with 1 tablespoon of sour cream.

Serve in soup dishes and add 1 teaspoon of sour cream pepper on top.

Jumbo Gumbo

4 tablespoons oil
2 tablespoons flour
1 pound raw shrimps, shelled and cleaned
½ pound fresh crabmeat
2 medium tomatoes
1 medium onion
1 clove garlic
½ cup cooked rice
3 cups fish broth
1 bay leaf
pinch red pepper
salt to taste

Put the oil in a saucepan and saute the shrimps for 5 minutes on each side. Remove shrimps and set aside. Repeat with crabmeat. Add onion, garlic and more oil if necessary. Cook until tender. Add the flour and mix in well. Slowly add the broth; when slightly thickened add shrimps, crabmeat, rice, bay leaf, red pepper and salt to taste. Simmer for 30 minutes. Serve with thick slices of French bread.

Meatball Minestrone

2 slices of bread
¼ cup cream
½ lb. chopped beef (raw)
1 small onion chopped fine
1 egg
1 teaspoon salt
¼ teaspoon pepper

Mix these ingredients thoroughly and roll into small balls. Set in refrigerator for two hours.

Meanwhile—

In soup kettle cook 1 package of frozen cut green beans, following instructions on package. Add 2 cans of beef consomme, 2 potatoes peeled and cut into medium size pieces. Scrape and slice 2 carrots, 1 coarsely chopped onion and 2 ribs of sliced celery. Simmer until vegetables are tender, about 15 minutes. Slice 1 large washed zucchini. Add zucchini to soup and drop in meatballs, simmer 30 minutes. Season to taste. Serve in deep bowls.

Stracciatella

This is truly an instant soup. It can be made with canned chicken broth and is surprisingly, effortlessly excellent.

Serves 6

4 cups simmering chicken broth
3 raw eggs
4 tablespoons freshly grated Parmesan cheese
   Salt and pepper
1 cup cold chicken broth
2 tablespoons parsley finely chopped for garnish

1. Bring 4 cups chicken broth to simmering point.
2. Combine eggs and cheese.
3. Stir cold chicken broth into egg combination.
4. Add cold mixture to hot broth stirring with a fork or wire whisk. (The eggs will form long strings.)
5. Simmer two minutes, adding salt and pepper to taste, and serve immediately, garnishing each bowl with parsley.

Super Bouillabaisse

¼ cup salad oil
3 tablespoons margarine
1 clove garlic, crushed
2 cups sliced onions
1 cup sliced green pepper
½ cup sliced celery
2 leeks, chopped
1 tablespoon salt
¼ teaspoon pepper
1½ teaspoon dried thyme leaves
⅛ teaspoon crumbled saffron
1 can (1 lb.) peeled tomatoes

Add all these ingredients into soup pot and saute, stirring about 1 minute.

Add 1 cup dry white wine, 1 can (10½) of tomato puree, then gently add

1 pound cod fillets, cut in half
1 pound haddock fillets, cut in half
1 pound peeled raw shrimp
4 tablespoons chopped parsley

Cover and cook gently 15 more minutes. Serve over toasted French Bread slices.

Cardinal Chicken Soup

Saute in 3 tablespoons butter, 1 tablespoon oil, 2 boneless, skinless chicken breasts cut into small pieces until tender, about 15 minutes. Remove Chicken, add 2 tablespoons flour and 1 teaspoon paprika. Remove from heat, stirring constantly add 2 cups chicken broth and 1 cup half milk and half cream. When smooth, season to taste and add 2 tablespoons of chopped parsley and chicken pieces.

Clam Soup French-Style

80 littleneck clams, the smaller the better
4 tablespoons butter
1 large onion, finely chopped
4 shallots, finely chopped
1 clove garlic, finely minced
1 teaspoon finely chopped fresh thyme or one-half teaspoon dried
1 tablespoon finely chopped fresh tarragon or 1 teaspoon dried
2 tablespoons flour
1 bottle dry white wine
2 cups heavy cream
2 egg yolks
Salt and freshly ground pepper
Tabasco sauce
Chopped chives

1. Rinse the clams under cold running water to remove all traces of sand from the shells.
2. Heat the butter in a large soup kettle and simmer the onion, shallots and garlic, stirring, until onion is wilted. Sprinkle with the thyme, tarragon and flour.
3. Add the wine, stirring constantly with a whisk. Simmer five minutes and add the clams. Cover and cook, stirring with a wooden spoon and shaking the kettle occasionally, until clams open, five to 10 minutes.
4. Add half the cream and stir. Blend remaining cream with the yolks and stir this into the soup. Cook over low heat almost to the boiling point. Do not let the soup boil or it may curdle. Taste to determine if the soup needs salt. If so, add it to taste. Add pepper and Tabasco. Serve in hot soup bowls with a sprinkling of chopped chives on top of each serving.

Yield: Eight or more servings.

American Bouillabaisse

5 cups fish stock
1 carrot
2 small onions
4 tablespoons oil
2 garlic cloves
1 pound codfish
8 scallops
8 large peeled shrimp, with tails
1 bay leaf
3 tomatoes
8 little neck clams, with shells
juice of 1 lemon
2 tablespoons sherry
salt and freshly ground black pepper

Peel and thinly slice the carrot and onions. Mince the garlic. Put the oil in a saucepan; when heated add the carrots, onion and garlic; sauté gently. Add the codfish, scallops, shrimp, fish stock, bay leaf, salt and pepper to the saucepan. Bring to a boil and simmer for 10 minutes. Cut the tomatoes in quarters, add to saucepan and simmer for 5 minutes. Add the lemon juice, little neck clams* and sherry; simmer for half an hour. Season to taste.

*The little necks will open while cooking in the soup, but leave shells in soup.

Jellied Cucumber

4 cucumbers, peeled, seeded and sliced
1 onion, sliced
1 teaspoon mixed pickling spices
5 cups water
1 tablespoon chopped parsley
2 envelopes unflavored gelatine
½ cup cold water
4 tablespoons sour cream
salt and freshly ground black pepper

Place the cucumber, onions, spices and water into the saucepan. Bring to a boil and simmer ½ hour. Pour through a sieve, pressing the cucumber through as much as possible. Take the soup and add the parsley, salt and pepper. Soften gelatine in ½ cup of cold water. Stir into the soup. Let soup cool and pour into a shallow pan to set. When soup has jelled, chop into small cubes and serve in champagne glasses with a dollop of sour cream.

Another Scallop Chowder

4 tablespoons of butter
1 teaspoon of dried thyme
1 sliced onion
2 sliced potatoes
1 sliced green pepper
2 cups peeled sliced tomatoes
4 cups hot water
2 lbs. Sea Scallops (cut in half)
2 teaspoons salt
½ teaspoon mace

Melt butter in soup kettle, add thyme, onions, potatoes, green pepper and saute slowly, moving around gently for 10 minutes. Add all other ingredients. Cover and simmer ½ hour. Do not boil. Add 1 cup heavy cream and check seasoning.

Gazpacho

2 cups beef broth
½ cup cucumber
½ cup celery
½ cup green pepper
1 cup tomatoes
¼ cup red onion
2 garlic buds
½ teaspoon tabasco
½ cup garlic croutons

Dice cucumber, celery, green pepper and tomatoes. Finely dice onion and garlic buds. Mix all the ingredients in a bowl, then cover and chill for 2 or 3 hours. Serve cold and garnish with croutons. (If you desire, you can put all the ingredients into a blender for 5 minutes on medium speed and then add the croutons.)

German Chowder

1 pound package sauerkraut
3 cups beef broth
1 onion, chopped fine
¼ pound mushrooms, sliced
4 beef frankfurters, sliced very thin
    so they will curl when cooked
¼ teaspoon paprika
   salt and pepper

Put all the ingredients in a saucepan and bring to a boil. Simmer 15 minutes, then add paprika. Salt and pepper to taste.

Real Beer Soup

2 12-ounce cans beer
1 tablespoon lemon juice
1 teaspoon salt
1 stick cinnamon
1 tablespoon flour
1 teaspoon sugar
few grains cayenne pepper

In small bowl put the flour and 3 tablespoons of beer until well mixed. In a saucepan, combine beer, lemon juice, sugar, salt, cinnamon and cayenne pepper. Bring to boiling point, <u>but do not boil</u>. Add flour mixture to soup and simmer gently for 5 minutes. Serve with warm pretzels.

Tuna Chowder

2 small cans tuna
3 tablespoons butter
1 tablespoon flour
1 medium-sized onion, chopped fine
2 medium-sized potatoes, peeled and cut in cubes
2 cups rich milk
2 cups water
1/8 teaspoon fennel seed
salt and pepper

Put potatoes into the water and bring to a boil. Cook until tender. Put the butter in a saucepan and when melted add the onion and cook until tender. Add the flour and mix well. Add the milk, tuna and potatoes plus the water that is left from the cooking. Add the fennel and seasonings. Important—this is a must to be made a day ahead, so tuna flavor can really set in.

Hummingbird Bean Soup

2 cups beef broth
2 cups canned red kidney beans
1 tablespoon oil
1 pound ground beef
1/2 teaspoon allspice
1/2 teaspoon chili powder
1/4 cup shredded cheddar cheese
salt and freshly ground black pepper

Put oil into a saucepan and cook chopped meat for 5 minutes. Add 1 cup of kidney beans and 2 cups of broth. Put 1 cup kidney beans into the blender for 1/2 minute and add to the soup. Then add the allspice and chili powder; season to taste. Simmer slowly for 20 minutes mixing well. Garnish with shredded cheese.

Wisconsin Cheese Soup

Serves 6 to 8.

2 tablespoons of butter
½ cup finely chopped onion
½ cup finely chopped green pepper
½ cup finely chopped celery
3 tablespoons of flour
5 cups fresh or canned chicken stock
½ pound cheddar cheese (coarsely grated)
1½ cups light cream
Salt and pepper to taste

In a 3 quart saucepan melt the butter, add onion, green pepper, and celery and cook 7 minutes. Mix in flour until all absorbed, slowly add chicken stock, beating constantly with wire whisk, until slightly thickened. A handful at a time add the cheese, beating constantly; add cream, bring to a boil, strain and season. Serve hot or cold.

French Mushroom Soup

1½ pounds fresh mushrooms—wash, dry and slice
¼ pound butter
2 finely chopped shallots
5 tablespoons flour
6 cups chicken stock
2 egg yolks ⎫
½ cup cream ⎬ cream together
salt and white pepper

Melt 4 tablespoons of butter, add mushrooms for 2 or 3 minutes tossing constantly. Transfer them to a dish.

In a soup pot melt remaining butter, remove pan and mix in flour until well mixed. Place back over heat and cook 2 minutes. Remove and cook a bit and add chicken stock. Bring to a boil stirring constantly. Add mushrooms and cook 15 minutes. Cool, put in blender for 1 minute. Return to pot, whisk some hot soup into egg cream and then return all to pot. Bring to a boil.

Old Fashion Borsch

1 medium carrot, cut into Julienne strips
3 medium beets, sliced
1 stalk celery, chopped
1 leek
1 pound corned beef
¼ pound salt pork
3 whole peppercorns
1 bay leaf
1 cup cabbage, shredded
1 teaspoon vinegar
½ cup sour cream
1 teaspoon chopped fresh dill
water

Put the salt pork in a saucepan and simmer until you have removed a lot of the fat. Remove the salt pork, add carrots, beets, celery and leek. Sauté for 10 minutes. Add the beef, peppercorns, bay leaf, cabbage and vinegar. Cover with water, cover the pan and cook until beef is tender. Remove beef and slice. Put the vegetables and water into the blender and purée. Pour back into the saucepan and heat. Put the meat slices into the soup. Garnish with sour cream and chopped fresh dill.

Rabbit Soup

1 rabbit, skinned, cleaned, washed and cut into pieces
4 tablespoons oil
½ cup oatmeal
2 onions, peeled and sliced
2 carrots, diced
2 parsnips, diced
2 sticks celery, diced
6 peppercorns
2 bay leaves
½ teaspoon herbs
1 ounce sherry wine

Put the oil into the saucepan, add the rabbit and onions and fry until golden brown. Add all the other ingredients but the sherry, cover with water and let simmer for 4 hours. Remove the meat and strain liquid. Throw away all the other ingredients. Cut the rabbit into small pieces and return to the liquid. Add the sherry and season to taste.

Artichoke Soup

    1 medium-size can artichoke bottoms
    1 medium onion
    4 tablespoons butter
    2 tablespoons flour
2½ cups chicken broth
    1 egg yolk
    ½ cup cream
    ½ orange rind, grated

Put 2 tablespoons of butter on to melt and add artichoke bottoms, sliced into slivers, with the finely sliced onion. Sauté gently for 10 minutes and then remove from pan. Put the remaining butter in pan to melt. Add the flour and mix well, slowly adding the chicken broth until it thickens slightly. Beat egg yolk and mix with the cream. Put 1 cup of hot broth into egg mixture, mix well and return it to the thickened broth. Add grated rind; salt and pepper if desired.

My Minestrone

⅛ pound salt pork
½ cup diced raw potatoes
½ cup diced raw carrots
½ cup diced raw turnip
½ cup diced raw cabbage
1 medium diced tomato
½ cup sliced zucchini
2 tablespoons chopped parsley
⅛ cup raw rice
1 quart beef broth
2 tablespoons tomato paste
½ teaspoon sage
4 teaspoons Parmesan cheese
   salt and freshly ground black pepper

Dice the salt pork and fry in a saucepan for a few minutes. Add all the vegetables and rice, sauté for 3 minutes. Pour the broth into the saucepan and simmer until vegetables are slightly tender and rice is cooked. Add tomato paste and seasonings. Simmer 2 more minutes. Sprinkle each serving with Parmesan cheese.

Super Oyster Stew

1 cup sliced mushrooms
20 small oysters in liquid
2 egg yolks
½ cup cream
3 cups rich milk
3 tablespoons butter
2 tablespoons flour
salt and freshly ground pepper

Melt the butter in a saucepan and add the mushrooms. Drain the oysters (save liquid) and sauté them with the mushrooms for 5 minutes. Then add the flour and mix well, but gently. Add the oyster liquid and milk until slightly thickened. Beat the egg yolks and blend <u>into</u> the soup and season to taste.

Pot Au Feu

1 small whole chicken
the liver, heart and giblets from **the chicken**
1 soup bone with meat, about 1 lb.
5 cups chicken broth
½ cup diced yellow turnip
¼ cup diced celery
1 small onion studded with whole clove
½ cup diced carrot
1 bouquet garni
8 slices toasted French bread
¼ cup freshly grated Parmesan cheese

Place chicken and bone in saucepan, cover with 5 cups of chicken broth and cook at low boiling point until meat is slightly tender. Add all the vegetables, liver, heart, giblets and the bouquet. Cook until vegetables are slightly tender; by this time the meat is done. Remove meat, cut into pieces and discard the bones. Remove the bouquet and the onion and discard. Garnish with slices of French bread toasted and sprinkled with Parmesan cheese.

Louisiana Gubmo

1 two-pound chicken, cut into 12 pieces
3 tablespoons oil
¾ cup onion, thinly sliced
1 cup fresh okra, thinly sliced
½ cup raw rice
¼ teaspoon thyme
1 cup fresh tomatoes, quartered
¼ cup Parmesan cheese
4 slices toasted French bread
   salt and freshly ground black pepper

Using a saucepan, saute the chicken pieces in the oil until brown on both sides, but not cooked. Remove from saucepan, add more oil if necessary, and saute tomatoes, onions, okra and rice. Put the chicken back into the saucepan and add 5 cups of water and the thyme. Boil gently ustil chicken is tender. Season to taste and garnish with slices of toasted French bread that has been sprinkled with Parmesan cheese.

Cauliflower Soup

1 small cauliflower
4 cups chicken broth
⅓ cup raw rice
¼ cup onion, finely chopped
½ teaspoon curry powder
1 tablespoon butter
⅓ cup heavy cream
   salt and finely ground pepper

Break up cauliflower into separate flowerettes. Put into chicken broth. Cover, bring to a boil and cook 15 minutes. Remove cauliflower from broth and set aside. Put rice into broth. Melt butter and saute onion and curry powder, then add to the broth, cover and cook 15 more minutes. Put broth in blender, blend 1 minute, put back in saucepan. Cut cauliflower into smaller pieces. Add to broth, stir in cream and add salt and fine ground pepper to taste. Note—if you would like cream of turnip, substitute cauliflower with peeled and diced white turnip. Cut turnip into about the same size pieces as cauliflower. Garnish with croutons.

Sausage Soup with Potato
(Great Meal)

Cut 1 lb. Kielbasa sausage into slices and fry in skillet.

Melt 4 tablespoons of butter to a soup pot add 2 cups finely chopped cabbage, 1 cup sliced thin onions and 1 cup sliced thin carrots. Saute 10 minutes. Add 2 cups beef consomme, 1 cup of water, the sausage, 2 tablespoons of vinegar, 1 tablespoon of salt and ½ teaspoon dried tarragon. Simmer gently until vegetables are tender.

Serve over small boiled potatoes.

Ravioli Soup

1 quart double strength chicken broth
½ pound frozen ravioli
½ cup grated fresh Parmesan cheese

Bring chicken broth to a boil—slip ravioli into the broth very gently. Boil for 20 minutes. Garnish with cheese.

Calcutta Soup

2 medium-size onions, sliced
4 tablespoons butter
2 teaspoons curry powder
2 medium size cans cream of chicken soup
½ cup cooked rice
1 cup half milk and half cream
salt and pepper

Saute onions in butter until tender, add curry powder and mix well. Add soup, milk, cream and rice. Season to taste. Serve hot.

Mulligatawny Soup

1 quart chicken broth
2 teaspoons salt
¼ cup mushrooms
¼ cup carrots
¼ cup celery
1 small clove garlic, chopped finely
¼ cup onions
2 teaspoons curry powder
2 tablespoons butter
½ cup heavy cream
1 cup cooked rice
salt and pepper

Put all the vegetables into the chicken broth and simmer 20 minutes. Place into blender and blend 2 minutes. Melt butter in a saucepan and add garlic, curry powder and seasonings. Saute 1 minute, then add flour and make a paste. Slowly add soup from the blender, cream and cooked rice. Simmer until hot, serve at once.

Bongo Bongo

8 fresh oysters
4 tablespoons fresh cooked spinach
½ cup cream
2 tablespoons butter
dash garlic salt
1 teaspoon A1 sauce
2 cups milk
1 tablespoon cornstarch
½ cup whipped cream
salt and pepper

Blend oysters, spinach, cream, butter, garlic salt and A1 sauce in blender. Blend 2 minutes. Heat milk (save ¼ cup for mixing with cornstarch). Add mixture from blender and bring gently to simmering point. Do not boil. Mix cornstarch in ¼ cup warm milk. Add to soup and mix in well, stirring constantly until thickened. Place in individual soup bowls, top each one with whipped cream and place under broiler. Broil 30 seconds—serve at once.

Our Mussel Soup

2 quarts mussels
½ cup white wine
½ cup water
1 teaspoon tarragon
2 tablespoons butter
½ cup cream
salt and freshly ground black pepper

Wash mussels thoroughly and place in a large kettle. Add the wine, water, and tarragon, cover and cook for 5 minutes. Leave covered for 10 more minutes. Remove the mussels from the broth and when they cool take the mussel from its shell. Place the mussels in a blender, add 2 tablespoons of butter, the broth, and ½ cup of cream. Blend ½ minute and put into the saucepan and heat. Salt and pepper to taste. Garnish with chopped parsley.

Captain's Bean Soup

2 cups black beans
3 quarts of water
1 bay leaf
1 ham bone
1 grapefruit
3 beef cubes
1 minced small green pepper
1 minced garlic clove
2 oz. dry sherry

Wash beans; cover with cold water; soak overnight, drain. Add 3 quarts water, bay leaf and ham bone. Boil gently until the beans are completely soft and the liquid fairly thick, add more water if necessary. Do not puree. Add the pulp from the grapefruit, beef cubes, green pepper, garlic and sherry. Simmer ½ hour.

Serve hot with bowl of rice, sprinkled with chopped fine raw onion.

Far East Pea Soup

1 cup fresh peas
1 small onion, diced
1 small carrot, diced
1 stalk celery, diced
1 potato, peeled and diced
1 teaspoon curry powder
3 cups chicken broth
1 cup cream
1/8 cup crushed peanuts
salt and freshly ground black pepper

Put peas, onions, carrots, potatoes, celery and 2 cups of the chicken broth in a covered saucepan and simmer for 15 minutes. Mix in blender for 1 minute. Put back into the saucepan and add 1 cup of chicken broth, cream; season to taste. Serve hot and garnish with a few crushed peanuts.

Duck Gumbo
(Very Special)

1 Duck, cut up into small pieces (have butcher chop up duck)
1/4 cup salt and pepper
1/4 cup flour
1/2 cup bacon drippings
1 large onion, chopped fine
2 large peeled tomatoes, cut up
3 tablespoons of flour
3 cups giblet water

Boil giblets in 4 cups of water to 1/2 hour and set aside.

Season duck pieces and roll each in flour, fry in bacon drippings until tender. About 10 minutes. Remove from pan add onions and tomatoes saute a few minutes. Add tablespoon of flour and stirring over heat with onions and tomatoes until flour all disappears. Add giblet water and duck, cook over low temperature for 2 hours. Taste for seasoning. Serve over rice.

Pumpkin Soup

Serves 6-8

1 tablespoon butter
2 cups cooked pumpkin (canned or fresh)
2½ cups chicken stock
2½ cups light cream
⅛ teaspoon ground cloves
½ teaspoon sugar
1 teaspoon lemon juice
2 drops Tabasco
½ teaspoon salt
¼ cup heavy cream (whipped)

In a heavy sauce pan melt butter over low heat, add pumpkin, chicken stock, cream, cloves, sugar, lemon juice, tabasco and salt. Blend all together thoroughly. Cook slowly 10 minutes. Pour through a sieve. Taste for salt and pepper. Chill well and add teaspoon of whipped cream per bowl.

Mom's Stew

2 lbs. lean beef stew meat
2 tablespoons bacon drippings
2 large onions, sliced thin
2 large white turnips, peeled, sliced thin
8 new, small potatoes, peeled
½ teaspoon garlic salt
1 medium can of peeled tomatoes
Salt and pepper to taste

Brown stew meat in bacon drippings, add turnips and cook slightly, add tomatoes and water, salt and pepper. Simmer 3 hours. 1 hour before cooking ends, add potatoes. When finished remove vegetables and meat to a platter.

Brown 2 tablespoons of butter in fry pan, add 2 tablespoons of flour, cream well, slowly add sauce for stew pot making a good gravy. Season to taste and pour over vegetables.

Lady Curzon Soup

2 cans turtle soup, warmed
1 teaspoon curry powder
4 tablespoons heavy cream
2 tablespoons brandy

Place the curry powder over a low heat, stirring constantly for 2 minutes. Warm the brandy in a metal measuring cup. Ignite the brandy and pour it over the curry powder. Extinguish the flame with the heavy cream. Add the warmed turtle soup and simmer a few minutes. Serve in demitasse cups.

Baked Steak Stew

2 lbs. round steak cut in 1" pieces
2 tablespoons of bacon drippings
2 cans of golden mushroom soup
½ cup water
½ cup sliced onions
½ teaspoon savory seasoning
1 pound of shelled peas
3 carrots, cut into 2" thin strips

Saute steak in bacon drippings. In casserole add soup, water, onions, meat and savory. Cover and bake at 350 for 1 hour. Open, add peas and carrots, cover and bake 1 hour more.

Meanwhile—

1½ cup bisquick } cream together
½ cup milk

Roll into oblong and sprinkle with ⅛ cup of chopped parsley. Roll up and slice in rounds. Place on top of stew. Brush with melted butter. Bake uncovered for 20 minutes.

Super Soup

    4 tablespoons oil
    1 medium onion, sliced
    1 stalk celery, sliced
    1 garlic clove
    3 sprigs parsley, chopped fine
    ½ cup tomato sauce, canned
    4 cups beef broth
    2 parsnips, peeled and sliced
    2 potatoes, peeled and sliced
    1 cup cauliflower, slice the flowerettes
    1 teaspoon fresh basil
      salt and freshly ground black pepper

Place the oil into a saucepan and sauté the onions, celery, parsley and garlic until tender. Add beef broth, parsnips, tomato sauce, potatoes, cauliflower and basil. Bring to a boil and cook until the vegetables are slightly tender. Season to taste.

Mrs. Goldberg's Chicken Soup

    4 pound chicken, whole
    2½ quarts water
    1 onion
    2 stalks celery
    6 sprigs parsley
    1 carrot
    1 leek
    1 parsley root
    2 cups cooked rice
      salt and pepper

Put chicken and water on to boil, including the liver, heart, etc. Cook ½ hour, then add rest of ingredients and salt and pepper. Cook slowly 1 hour; strain and cool. Remove all chicken from bones and put meat in soup. Leave soup in refrigerator overnight; next day skim and heat and serve over cooked rice.

Consommé Diable

¾ cup cream sauce
¼ cup grated Parmesan cheese
8 slices French bread
4 cups hot canned consommé
dash of cayenne pepper

(Cream sauce—1 tablespoon butter melted in saucepan, add 1 tablespoon of flour and mix well. Slowly add ¾ cup of milk and cook until it thickens)

Mix cream sauce, cheese and cayenne pepper together. Spread over both sides of French bread and place on baking sheet. Broil in oven 5 minutes and turn over. Broil 5 minutes more. Place in individual soup bowls and pour hot consommé over bread.

Jellied Madrilene

Serves 6

3 cans chicken broth
2 cans tomato puree
4 envelopes unflavored gelatin
½ cup water or white wine
2 tablespoons chives chopped
½ lemon sliced for garnish

1. Combine chicken broth and tomato puree in a saucepan. Simmer for ten minutes.
2. Pour cold water into another saucepan.
3. Sprinkle gelatin on the surface of the water. Add a few more drops of water to dampen gelatin if powdery crystals remain on the surface.
4. Allow gelatin to stand undisturbed for five minutes.
5. Place gelatin over gentle heat until dissolved.
6. Add gelatin to broth.
7. Chill four hours in the refrigerator.
8. Garnish with chives and sliced lemon.

Claret Consommé

1 cup Claret wine
2 cinnamon sticks
1 tablespoon sugar
3 cups beef broth
4 slices lemon

Put the Claret, cinnamon sticks and sugar into a saucepan, bring to a boil. When boiling remove from the heat, cover and let stand for 6 hours. Strain into beef broth and simmer until very hot. Garnish with sliced lemon.

Pacific Oyster Stew

4 tablespoons soft butter
1½ pints light cream
1½ pints Pacific Oysters and their liquid
   fresh ground pepper
   salt to taste
1 tablespoon chopped parsley

Poach oysters in their liquid over low heat, 2 or 3 minutes—add butter, cream, salt and pepper. Heat gently. Sprinkle with parsley.

Basque Consommé

2 medium size cans consommé
⅓ cup julienne strips green pepper
½ cup peeled and seeded tomatoes, diced
⅓ cup cooked rice
1 teaspoon chopped, fresh chervil
1 tablespoon chopped parsley
   salt and pepper

Put consommé in saucepan adding 1 can of water. Add all other ingredients but parsley, cook 10 minutes. Season to taste, garnish with parsley.

Teriyaki Soup

2 lbs. lean stew meat cut into tiny pieces. Saute in ¼ cup peanut oil, when brown add 1 stalk celery, 1 carrot, 1 bay leaf, 1 onion. Cover with water, cover pan and cook slowly until meat is tender. About 30 minutes remove vegetables and bay leaf. Add 1 small can drained peas, 1 small can drained tiny carrots, 1 small can crushed pineapple, 1 tablespoon worcestershire sauce, 2 tablespoons sherry wine and 1 pound washed, dried and sliced fresh mushrooms. Cook ten minutes.

Mix 3 tablespoons of cornstarch with 3 tablespoons of water, slowly add to hot soup. Check seasoning.

Hearty Lima Bean

- ½ pound package dried lima beans
- 1 quart water
- 1 teaspoon salt
- 1 left-over ham bone
- 2 stalks celery and tops, sliced
- 1 medium onion, chopped
- 1 tablespoon chopped parsley
- 1 bay leaf
- ⅛ teaspoon ground thyme
- ½ teaspoon Accent
- ½ cup croutons
- salt and pepper

Combine beans, water, salt, ham bone, celery, onions, parsley and bay leaf in saucepan. Bring to a boil and simmer 1 hour. Remove bone; pick off any meat and add to soup. Simmer 20 minutes longer. Season to taste. Serve with croutons.

Mrs. Goldberg's Chowder

3 tablespoons butter
1 onion, chopped finely
2 tablespoons flour
4 cups water
1½ pound halibut, cubed
3 potatoes, peeled and cubed
1 cup heavy cream
4 slices smoked salmon, cubed
2 tablespoons chopped chive
salt and pepper

Melt the butter in a saucepan and sauté onions 5 minutes. Sprinkle in flour and mix well. Add water slowly, then add the fish and potatoes and cook slowly for 30 minutes. Add the cream and salmon; season to taste. Garnish with chopped chives.

Tomato Consomme

This is a thin tomato soup. A good choice for serving before a large steak dinner.

Serves 6.

1 16-oz. can peeled tomatoes
3 cans chicken broth
½ teaspoon allspice
½ teaspoon thyme
1 teaspoon basil
1 bay leaf
1 teaspoon lemon juice
1 teaspoon tomato paste
2 tablespoons sherry or Madeira
2 tablespoons freshly chopped parsley for garnish

1. Drain tomatoes.
2. Place tomatoes, broth, herbs, lemon juice and tomato paste in a saucepan.
3. Cover and simmer twenty minutes.
4. Strain and return to the saucepan.
5. Add sherry or Madeira.
6. Serve hot with a garnish of freshly chopped parsley.

Real French Onion Soup

3 large onions, thinly sliced
3 tablespoons butter
1 tablespoon flour
3 cups beef broth, double strength
4 slices toasted French bread
4 slices Gruyère cheese

Melt the butter in a saucepan and sauté the onions slowly, until they are a rich brown color. Mix in the flour and then slowly add the beef broth. Simmer for 30 minutes, until it reaches a rich color. Season to taste. Pour soup in oven-bake dishes. Place a piece of toasted French bread on top of the soup and cover with thin slices of Gruyère cheese. Place under broiler until the cheese starts to melt.

Leek and Potato Soup

2 leeks
4 tablespoons butter
4 cups chicken broth
2 medium-size potatoes
1 small ham bone
1 cup milk
½ cup heavy cream
⅛ teaspoon ground mace
salt and pepper

Chop leeks and cook in butter. Add stock, peeled and sliced potatoes and the ham bone. Cover, bring to a boil and cook until the potatoes are very tender. Remove bone and put the soup into the blender. Blend 2 minutes. Add milk and cream; season to taste. Serve hot or cold and garnish with ground mace.

Holiday Sweet Soup

1 cup dried apricots
1 cup dried prunes
1 quart apple cider
2 tablespoons sugar
juiced 1 lemon
1/4 teaspoon ground cinnamon
1/4 teaspoon nutmeg
dash of ground clove

Wash apricots and prunes. Dry. Combine cider and dried fruits and heat to boiling. Lower heat and simmer for 30 minutes. Add sugar, lemon juice, spices and salt.

Serve hot, garnish with a lemon slice (good cook also serves with Sour Cream).

Bean and Almond Soup

1/2 cup navy beans
3 cups chicken broth
3/4 cup blanched almonds
2 large leeks
1 garlic clove
1 teaspoon sugar
1/2 cup white wine
1/2 cup sour cream
salt and freshly ground black pepper

Cover the beans in enough water and soak overnight. Drain the beans and cook them in the chicken broth until they are tender. Crush the almonds in a blender or pound them in a mortar. Stir the almonds into the beans. Add the finely chopped leeks, crushed garlic, sugar and wine. Season to taste. Cook 10 more minutes, then put through a strainer or serve as is. Garnish with 1 teaspoon of sour cream in each bowl.

Escoffier Onion Soup

¼ pound Margarine
2½ pounds sliced onions
5 cups beef bouillion
2 tablespoons of Escoffier sauce
1 bay leaf
1½ teaspoons celery salt
1 teaspoon black pepper

Heat margarine in soup pot, add sliced onions and brown very well stirring constantly. Add beef bouillon, escoffier sauce, bay leaf, celery salt and pepper. Simmer 40 minutes, remove bay leaf. Salt to taste.

Serve with toasted French bread slices and sprinkle well with grated parmesan cheese.

Peasant's Broth

3 large onions, thinly sliced
2 tablespoons oil
1 tablespoon flour
½ cup dry white wine
4 cups beef broth, boiling
4 slices stale rye bread
½ cup freshly grated Gruyère

Using a saucepan, simmer onions in oil until pale, golden color. Sprinkle with flour and stir well; add wine. Remove from heat and add boiling broth. Place 1 slice of stale rye bread in soup bowls, sprinkle with cheese and pour soup into bowls.

Mom's Chicken Soup

1 four pound chicken, cut into 10 pieces
3 chopped carrots
3 chopped stalks of celery
1 chopped onion
6 cups cold water
1½ cups cooked thin noodles
chopped parsley

Place 1st five ingredients in soup pot. Cover and cook slowly for two hours. Cool place in refrigerator over night. Skim. Add cooked noodles and parsley and heat to hot.

Old English Cheese Soup

½ cup butter
4 tablespoons flour
4 cups milk
1 pound Old English cheese
1½ tablespoons Worcestershire sauce
½ teaspoon paprika
4 rusks

Melt butter in a saucepan, add flour, and mix. Slowly add milk and cook until thickened. Add cheese, Worcestershire sauce and paprika and cook over very low heat until cheese is well blended. Salt and pepper to taste. Serve with rusks.

Country Minestrone

6 cups beef broth
1 tablespoon oil
1 onion, sliced
1 tomato, diced
½ pound fresh green string beans
1 fresh leek, diced
1 potato, peeled and diced
1 small zucchini, sliced
½ cup canned kidney beans
½ cup raw elbow macaroni
1 garlic clove, chopped finely
1 teaspoon basil
1 tablespoon Parmesan cheese
salt and fresh ground black pepper

Sauté the onion in the oil and add the tomato. Then add the broth, string beans, leek, potato, zucchini and kidney beans. Cook to a full boil. When vegetables are slightly cooked, add elbow macaroni and cook 10 minutes more. In a side dish mix basil, garlic and cheese, and add to the soup. Bring to a boil and remove from the heat. Season to taste and serve at once.

Index

Almond Cream Soup	12	Consommé, Tomato	58
Apple and Banana Soup	29	Crab Soup Surrey	24
Artichoke Soup	45	Crab Soup, The	15
Asparagus Soup, Spring	20	Creme Germiny	8
Avocado Soup, Easy	15	Cucumber Soup, Cold with Mint	21
		Cucumber Soup, Hasty	29
Bean and Almond Soup	60	Cucumber, Jellied	40
Bean Soup, Captain's	50		
Bean Soup, Hummingbird	42	Early Spring Soup	18
Bean Soup, White	35	Fruit Soup, Mama's	23
Beer Soup, Real	42		
Bisque, Southern	11	Gazpacho	41
Bongo Bongo	49	Gazpacho, New York	22
Borsch, Old Fashion	44	Greek Lemon Soup	12
Borsch, Quickie Cold	30	Gumbo, Duck	51
Bouillabaisse, American	40	Gumbo, Jumbo	37
Bouillabaisse, Super	38	Gumbo, Louisiana	47
Broccoli Soup	10	Holiday Sweet Soup	60
Broth, Beef	6	Hollandaise Soup	31
Broth, Chicken	6		
Broth, Fish	7	Jellied Madrilène	55
Broth, Peasant's	61	Kaassoep	35
Broth, Vegetable	7		
		Lady Curzon Soup	53
Caldo Gallego	13	Laurent Soup	36
Cherry, Swedish	10	Leafy Green Soup	19
Chicken Soup, Almond	18	Leek and Potato Soup	59
Chicken Soup, Cardinal	39	Lima Bean Soup, Hearty	57
Chicken Soup, Cold Curried and Pea	29	Lobster Stew	24
Chicken Soup, Green Mountain	20	Minestrone, Country	62
Chicken Soup, Mom's	61	Minestrone, Meatball	37
Chicken Soup, Mrs. Goldberg's	54	Minestrone, My	45
Chicken Soup, Quick Indian	24	Mom's Stew	52
Calcutta Soup	48	Mulligatawny Soup	49
Callaloo Soup	27	Mushroom Creme, Fresh	16
Carrot and Leek Soup	30	Mushroom Soup, Clear	12
Carrot Soup, Iced	25	Mushroom Soup, French	43
Cauliflower Soup	47	Mussel Soup, Our	50
Caviar Soup, Swedish	11		
Celery Velouté	8	Napolean Soup, a la	16
Champagne and Crab Soup	21	Onion Soup, Escoffier	61
Cheese Soup, Old English	62	Onion Soup, Real French	59
Cheese Soup, Wisconsin	43	Oyster, Quick Chesapeake and Chicken	35
Chowder, Another Scallop	41	Oyster Stew, Pacific	56
Chowder, Cape Cod Clam	13	Oyster Stew, Super	46
Chowder, Corn with a Twist	36		
Chowder, German	41	Pea Soup Diable	21
Chowder, Haddock	14	Pea Soup, Far East	51
Chowder, Mrs. Goldberg's	58	Pea Soup, Summer	33
Chowder, Tuna	42	Petite Marmite	19
Clam Broth, Jellied	30	Pot au Feu	46
Clam Soup, Easy	16	Potage Chantilly	33
Clam Soup, French Style	39	Pumpkin Soup	52
Clam Stew	17		
Consommé, Aurora	32	Rabbit Soup	44
Consommé, Basque	56	Ravioli Soup	48
Consommé, Claret	56	Salad Soup, Molly's Left Over	17
Consommé, Diable	55	Salmon Bisque	26
Consommé, Frosted	26	Salmon Mousse, Summer	28
Consommé, New York Clam	32	Sausage Soup with Potato	48
Consommé, Spinach	15	Scallop Soup, Cape	34

Serendipity	36	Turkey Soup, Smoked	28
Sherry Soup	14	Vegetable Soup, Farmhouse	22
Steak Stew, Baked	53	Vegetable Soup, "No Time"	11
Stracciatella	38	Vichyssoise, Carrot	9
Super Soup	54	Vichyssoise, Chilled Cream	27
Super Soup, Quick	18		
Swiss Cheese Soup, Old Fashion	33	Watercress Corn Soup	23
		Watercress Soup	25
Teriyaki Soup	57	Watercress Soup, Summer	27
Tomato Soup, Chilled Garden	32	Won Ton Soup	34
Tomato Soup, Creamy Cold	31		
Tomato Soup, Madrid	9	Yoghurt Soup	26